What Makes a Roller Coaster Roll?

and other ways science makes the funfair fun

By Paul Mason

Contents

T0345656

All the fun of the fair

Being flung is fun!

Whether you want to be flung up, down or sideways, there's a funfair ride for the job. Reverse bungees fling you up in the air. Drop towers plummet down to earth at breakneck speed. Screaming swings swoop you wildly from side to side.

What makes a funfair ride fun?

Forces, that's what! These pushes and pulls fling you from side to side and up and down. To understand how this works, you'll need to ask a scientist. The best one to ask would be Sir Isaac Newton. This famous fellow knew more about the forces that move objects around than just about anyone, ever. In fact, he came up with the First Law of Motion: *An object stays still, or carries on moving with the same speed or direction, unless a force acts on it.*

That sounds a bit dry and dusty! But actually, as you'll discover, every funfair ride ever built has relied on Newton's First Law.

The biggest, most popular ride at the funfair is always the roller coaster. So that's where our investigation into funfair forces will start.

Name: **Sir Isaac Newton**

Dates: 1642–1727

Job: Britain's most brilliant scientist ever!

Sir Isaac was a famous grumpy-guts, and liked nothing more than to lock himself in his laboratory for days on end doing experiments. It is said that he stuck needles in his eye sockets to see how it affected his vision. When he got bored of studying this, Sir Isaac began studying how forces make things move. He was especially interested in planets and comets – but his work applies to ALL objects. Even funfair rides.

Newton became hooked on forces by going to the fair. It looks a bit tame compared to fairs today!

Strange...

As well as being Britain's greatest scientist, one story says that Sir Isaac invented the cat flap. When his cat had kittens, he built another, smaller cat flap for the kittens. It didn't occur to him that they would follow their mother through the large cat flap – which goes to show that Sir Isaac might have been a genius, but he wasn't all that practical.

...but true

The need for speed

Faster than a car!

Roller coasters carry people up steep climbs, whoosh back down the other side, and whiz through tight bends. The fastest roller coasters zoom along at over 160 kph – faster than most cars can go! Amazingly, though, they don't even have an engine.

What makes a roller coaster roll?

Without an engine, what force makes a roller coaster move and how do they *keep* rolling? The answer lies at the top of the **lift hill**. This is where a roller coaster gathers all the energy that moves it along.

Top 5: Record-setting roller coasters

 1 The first wheeled roller coaster (France) was in 1817.

 2 The first loop in a roller coaster (Centrifugal Railway in France) was in 1846.

3 The fastest (Formula Rossa in Abu Dhabi) travels at 240 kph (150 mph).

4 The longest (Steel Dragon in Japan) is 2.5 km (1.5 miles).

5 The biggest drop (Sheikra, USA) is 61 metres (200 feet) straight down.

Fighting gravity

The roller coaster is dragged up the lift hill on a toothed rail in the middle of the track. The toothed rail is playing tug-of-war with a force called gravity. Gravity is a force that constantly pulls all objects downward, toward the centre of Earth. To move the roller coaster up, the rail must be pulling with more force than gravity.

Ready to roll

When the roller coaster reaches the top of the lift hill, it balances there for a split second. At this moment, it is brimming with **potential energy***. It is like a pulled-back catapult. This energy is going to power it through the rest of the ride.

Force of toothed rail pulling up

POTENTIAL ENERGY

Force of GRAVITY

For a split second, the roller coaster balances at the top of the lift hill. It is ready to plunge down the other side.

*Like the potential energy of the drop tower on pages 20–21.

Faster and faster

Let the fun begin!

Of course, grinding slowly up a lift hill isn't the exciting part of a roller-coaster ride. It is what happens next that shows how forces really make things fun!

How does a roller coaster pick up speed?

As the front half of the roller coaster goes over the top of the lift hill, the force of gravity begins to pull it downward. The rear part of the roller coaster then starts to be pulled over the hill – both by gravity and by the front half, which is picking up speed. As more of the roller coaster is pulled over the top of the hill, its speed increases.

GRAVITY

As more carriages cross the hill, gravity pulls more on the downhill side and less on the uphill.

A higher lift hill is better because even when the *whole* roller coaster is over the hill, it still keeps accelerating. Gravity keeps pulling it to faster and faster speeds until some other force slows the roller coaster down.

Try this!

Want to understand why roller coaster designers like high lift hills?

What you need:

- a skateboard
- a safe slope (NOT on the road or anywhere cars might come)
- chalk
- a long measuring tape
- a friend

What to do:

1 Use the chalk to write 'Spot 1' about halfway up the slope.

2 Put the skateboard down on the spot, sit on it, and roll straight down. Where the skateboard stops, write 'Finish 1'.

3 Repeat the process for 'Spot 2', 3 metres further up the slope.

4 Measure the gaps between Spots 1 and 2, and Finishes 1 and 2.

5 What do you notice? Is the distance the same as between Spots 1 and 2, or different?

Hint: the skateboard goes further when it starts from a higher spot because the force of gravity can then work on it for longer. However, it does not go three metres extra.*

*Turn to pages 10 and 11 to understand why.

Round the bend

More in store

Plunging downhill off the lift hill is exciting, but the roller coaster has plenty more thrills in store. When the roller coaster gets to the bottom of the lift hill, it nearly always goes steeply upward again. Then the roller coaster will probably start wiggling from side to side. Before your ride is finished, you'll have been squashed, stretched and thrown sideways by a variety of forces.

How come the roller coaster doesn't just fly off the tracks?

Remember Sir Isaac's First Law! *An object ... carries on moving with the same speed or direction unless a force acts on it.* The reason why the roller coaster not flying off the tracks is the tracks themselves. They push against the roller coaster's wheels and force it to change direction.*

The tracks push against the wheels.

The roller coaster wants to go straight on.

*A bit like when dodgems collide. See pages 16–17.

TOP SECRET

To: Phileas H DeWitt
From: Agent X
Subject: Screamer Ride
Date: April 1, 1930

Sir,

I have now completed my investigation into the Screamer Ride at Billy Budd's Fairground. The secret of the ride is its special wheels. These do NOT work in the same way as railway wheels.

The Screamer Ride has wheels above, below and to the side of the tracks. This allows the carriages to go round corners at speeds that would tip a normal railway carriage over.

Armed with this information, it should be possible to build a roller coaster of your own, to bring the crowds back to DeWitt's Fantastic Funfair.

Strange...

In many languages, roller coasters are known as 'Russian Mountains'. This is because in the 1400s, Russians started building rides on steep, ice-covered slopes. People paid to slide down the icy hill in carriages. Strangely, the Russian for roller coaster is *amerikanski ropa* – or 'American slides'.

...but true

Slowing to a stop

Stealing your speed

Roller coasters don't have brakes so what slows them down at the end of the ride? The answer is that forces are constantly stealing the roller coaster's speed and slowing it down.

Gravity minuses and pluses

As the roller coaster races uphill, gravity tries to pull it backward. This slows it down. Of course, the roller coaster then goes back downhill again on the other side, picking up speed again. The roller coaster could keep going forever if gravity was the only force involved – but it's not.

How come friction's such a drag?

As the wheels of the roller coaster roll along, they encounter a force called friction. Friction pulls on objects that rub against each other, slowing them down. If you fall over and slide to a stop when ice-skating, it's friction that slows you down and stops you from whamming full-speed into the barriers. The same happens to the roller coaster. The friction of the wheels against the rails is constantly slowing the roller coaster down and taking away a little bit of its speed.

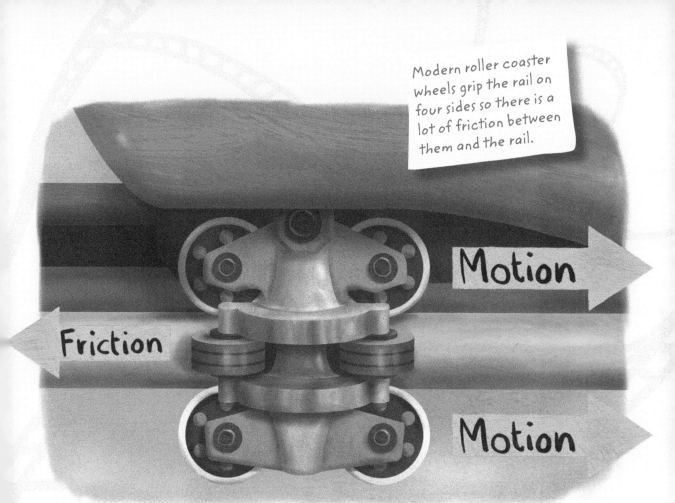

Modern roller coaster wheels grip the rail on four sides so there is a lot of friction between them and the rail.

Motion

Friction

Motion

You never know how much friction a material will generate unless you've done an experiment to check. There are some basic guidelines, though:

1. Rougher surfaces generally create more friction than smooth ones. Sandpaper makes more friction than glass.

2. A large area rubbing against something else will generate more friction than a small one.

3. The harder two surfaces press against each other, the more friction they generate.

Hair resistance!

Hair horrors!

The funfair is a terrible place to visit if you're fussy about your hair. Riding a 100 kph roller coaster is like going out in a strong gale. No wonder it's bad for your hairstyle!

Why is the funfair so hard on hair?

It's all because of a force called air resistance. Wind is the air moving around you but air resistance, which feels like wind, is caused by you moving through the air. As you push against the air the air pushes back. Of course, in a roller coaster, you're solid and heavy – and strapped into your seat – so the push of the air can't move you at all. As your hair is flimsy and light, the air doesn't have any trouble pushing that around!

Air pushes back

The roller coaster and passengers push through air

Strange...

Air resistance means there is a maximum speed at which an object can fall. For humans, this is about 200 kph – which is fast enough to kill you if you hit the ground. No wonder an object's maximum falling speed is called its 'terminal **velocity**'.

... but true

What other effects does air resistance have?

Air resistance is one of the key things that slow down funfair rides. It's particularly important on a roller coaster, which doesn't have an engine to fight back against the force of air resistance. Modern roller coasters often have an **aerodynamic** shape to reduce the effect of air resistance as much as possible.

Air Flow

Car slides through air

Air Flow

Air Flow

Air Flow

Car bashes through air

You feel more air resistance the faster you go. Test it on your bicycle. On a wind-free day, start cycling slowly in your easiest gear. You feel a gentle breeze on your face. The force of air resistance is weak, because you are not travelling very fast. Now **accelerate** to maximum speed. You will feel a strong wind in your face. Because you are travelling faster, the force of air resistance has increased.

Claim your coconut

Nothing could be simpler than throwing a ball – right?

You might think winning a coconut is just a matter of throwing a ball and knocking it off its perch but it's nothing *like* as simple as that. It's actually very complicated, because of all the different forces involved.

Can Sir Isaac help?

As a matter of fact, he can. Sir Isaac spent years discovering how objects move through space. All you have to do is remember which forces are involved:

1. The force of your throw, as the muscles in your arm launch the wooden ball at the coconut.
2. Gravity, which wants to pull the ball downward.
3. Air resistance, which will slow the ball's forward motion.
4. On a windy day, you may need to add a fourth factor: the force of the wind may push your ball off-course.

So ... what's the best way to knock a coconut off its perch?

You need to minimize the effects of the various forces on your throw, apart from the force of your arm. This makes it more likely that your ball will hit the target. The photo opposite shows two options. See if you can work out which is better. (The answer is at the bottom of page 15.)

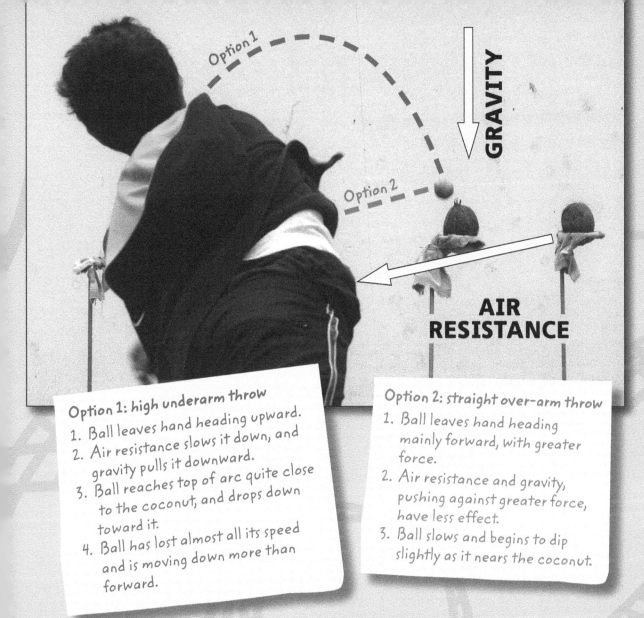

GRAVITY

AIR RESISTANCE

Option 1

Option 2

Option 1: high underarm throw
1. Ball leaves hand heading upward.
2. Air resistance slows it down, and gravity pulls it downward.
3. Ball reaches top of arc quite close to the coconut, and drops down toward it.
4. Ball has lost almost all its speed and is moving down more than forward.

Option 2: straight over-arm throw
1. Ball leaves hand heading mainly forward, with greater force.
2. Air resistance and gravity, pushing against greater force, have less effect.
3. Ball slows and begins to dip slightly as it nears the coconut.

Strange...

Some of the earliest investigations of gravity happened in 1589 at the Leaning Tower of Pisa. A scientist called Galileo dropped different-sized stone balls from the top to see if heavier ones fell faster (they didn't). It must have come as a shock to passing tourists having to dodge Galileo's stones!

...but true

Answer: Throwing straight and fast is the better way to hit the coconut. The ball travels faster and over a shorter distance. Gravity, air resistance and the wind have less effect on your throw.

Be a dodgem demon

If there's one ride you almost always have to wait to get on, it's the dodgems. However, once you're on the rink, trying to crash into your friends, what's the best attack strategy? The science of forces will help you decide.

Dodgem tactics

There are three basic tactics for ramming into someone out on the dodgem rink.

Tactic 1: Head-on collision

This will only be successful if you are going faster than the other car. If you hit each other head-on at the same speed, the two cars crash together with equal force and stop moving.

Tactic 2: Stealth attack

The trouble with this approach is that you will be adding to your victim's speed! With the other car already moving forward, the force of your hit will cause it to move even *faster* – which could prove dangerous for you later.

Tactic 3: Side-on collision

An attack from the side will give your victim a mighty knock if you are going fast enough. You might even shock their foot to come off the accelerator pedal – then they'll be a sitting duck!

IMPACT!

Of course, you want to hit your friends hard, but not so hard that their teeth fall out! That's why dodgem cars have rubber strips around them.

Strips squash down, absorbing some of the force. Next, the strips will spring back into their old shape.

You need my Second Law of Motion to find out the best dodgem tactic! The first bit of this says: *Any change in a body's motion is related to the force with which it is moved* ... So hitting a dodgem at full speed (with maximum force) will knock it further off-course. For a really *excellent* ram, however, the next bit of my Second Law of Motion is important: ... *and will always happen in the same direction as that force is applied.* So if you hit the other car from the side, it will be knocked sideways!

Dropping!

Drop to your death – and live!

Do you want to know what it feels like to drop to your death from 100 metres up in the air and live to tell your friends about it? Take a ride on a drop tower!

What on earth is a drop tower?

It's a ride that hoists you steadily up to the top of a tall tower. It leaves you there for a moment or two to admire the view and realise just how terrifyingly high up you are. Then it releases and drops you plummeting to the ground.

Top 5: Drop tower extremes

1. The tallest Drop Tower (Giant Drop in Australia) is 119 metres high.

2. The fastest Drop Tower (Giant Drop again!) reaches speeds of 135 kph (84 mph).

3. The highest (Big Shot, USA) is only 48 metres tall but it's on top of a 281 metre tall building. The top is 329 metres above the ground, making it the longest drop in the world.

4. Supreme Scream (USA) is a turbo drop tower, which accelerates riders up the tower *and* back down again. They experience four times the force of gravity during the ride.

5. The tallest Space Shot* tower (*La Veganza del Enigma* Spain) is 115 metres high.

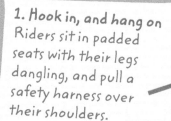

1. Hook in, and hang on
Riders sit in padded seats with their legs dangling, and pull a safety harness over their shoulders.

2. Going up ...
The seats are all pulled upward. This must be by a force greater than gravity, which is trying to pull them down.

3. Aaah! Coming down
Once the seats are released, gravity can take over. The riders plummet back to earth, gravity pulling them faster and faster.

4. And relax
Just as the ride is about to crash, the ride stops. Powerful magnets are used to slow and then stop it.

MAGNETIC FORCE

MAGNETIC FORCE

*See page 20 for more details on this death-defying ride.

Just falling is boring!

All aboard? Going down...

If you think just falling from the top of a drop tower sounds dull, don't worry. There are a couple of even *more* terrifying drop tower rides you can try: the Turbo Drop, and the Space Shot.

What's a space shot?

This is a ride that uses **compressed air** to pull the riders up the tower. The air blows into a central column that is a giant **piston**. As the piston moves down, the riders travel up at about 20 kph – *much* faster than on a normal drop tower. Then they bump back down in a drop-stop, drop-stop rhythm, as an air valve at the top of the piston opens and closes.

As the air starts to build up inside the piston, it wants to expand – like when you blow up a balloon. The forces of gravity and air pressure together become greater than the force of gravity acting on the riders. The piston drops down, and the riders rise up. When the valve opens and air is released, the riders drop down again.

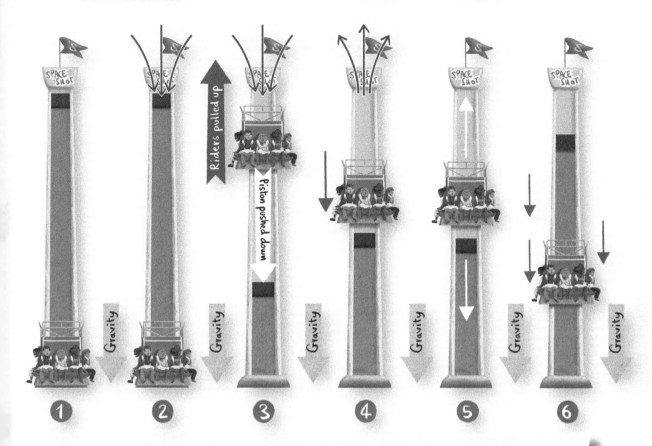

How the Space Shot works

1. Riders climb aboard and strap in.
2. Compressed air injected into central column.
3. Air pushes piston downward, which pulls riders up.
4. Air released, allowing carriage to drop suddenly.
5. Valve is closed, air compresses and riders stop falling.
6. Valve opened and closed again, allowing riders to return to ground.

And a Turbo Drop tower?

This tower is probably the scariest drop tower of all. The designers of this one didn't think the downward pull of gravity from the top of the tower was enough. They decided to add another force. Compressed air pushes the riders back down to the ground. They are fired downward like peas shooting out of a peashooter.

The Screaming Swing

Thrills – but hopefully no spills

If you enjoyed the Space Shot, perhaps you'd like to try another ride that uses gravity and compressed air to make you scream? If so, it's time to head over to the Screaming Swing.

What's a screaming swing?

This is a ride where two carriages hang from solid arms. When everyone's on board, the operator pushes a button, and a squirt of compressed air pushes the arms. The carriages swing forward and back, then forward again. Each time they swing forward, the arms get another push of compressed air. With each push, they swing a bit higher, like a child being pushed on a swing in the park.

Arm pulls carriage back

Carriage wants to pull away

The Screaming Swing is powered by compressed air.

Push forces arm forward

Why will it make me scream?

Some screaming swings reach an angle of 120°. That's not *actually* upside down (that would be 180°), but it *feels* like upside down. On top of that, the swing travels at up to 100 kph. As the swing travels in a circular motion, people are pressed into their seats by what is called centrifugal force*.

Try this!

Want to prove that compressed air can generate force?

What you need:

- various balloons (including long, thin ones)

- a plastic straw

- string

- sticky tape

- a tape measure

What to do:

1 Tape the straw to the balloons, then put the string through the straw. Stretch the string between two solid objects, such as a door handle and a heavy chair, pull it tight and tie it off.

2 Blow up the balloon so it's full of air, but don't tie the end – just pinch it closed so air can't escape.

3 Pull the straw all the way back to one end of the string, and then tape the balloon to it.

4 Let go, and let your air-powered straw whiz along the string. Measure how far it travels.

Hint: using a fishing line or a shorter straw will affect the amount of friction slowing down the balloon; different-shaped balloons will meet greater or smaller amounts of air resistance.

*Find out more about this on pages 28–31.

The Waltzer - sick bag at the ready!

Old, but good

In among all the modern, high-tech funfair rides is the Waltzer, an old favourite, and one that has been making people sick since it first appeared in 1933.

How does the Waltzer work?

The Waltzer is like a carousel, but it's way faster and a lot scarier. The carts move in a circular direction around a central point. At the same time, they can spin round and round and, as the floor of the ride is not flat, they go up and down.

Can you identify the forces that push and pull the carts around? The answers are at the bottom of page 25.

Why does the Waltzer make people sick?

There are so many different forces involved in a waltzer. Humans are built to handle changes of direction, but only really one at a time. Riders on a waltzer feel that they're being pushed and pulled, up and down, round and round, forwards and backwards, and all within a few seconds. Their senses of balance and vision get confused. Most of us just get dizzy, but some people's bodies decide they must have been poisoned. Their body then automatically vomits to try and get rid of the 'poison' (which isn't really there at all).

Strange...

If you start to feel sick on a funfair ride, try these cures:
- close your eyes,
- look at the **horizon**,
- eat ginger.

...but true

Answers:
1. A waltzer floor is pushed around by an electric engine.
2. The attendant spins the cars.
3. Gravity helps the cars to spin as they go down the slope, as the weight inside them is pulled downward.
4. Gravity also helps the cars to spin as they go up the slope.

Reverse bungee

Better than a bungee

In a bungee jump, you jump downward and ping back up on the end of an elastic rope. Then you boing up and down again until you're left dangling helpless in the air, like a spent yo-yo. A reverse bungee is less terrifying, and MUCH more fun.

How does a reverse bungee work?

First, you climb into a **spherical** cage and sit down (some cages hold more than one person). Your seat is able to spin around inside the cage. The cage is anchored to the ground using a powerful **electromagnet**. Two giant telescopic arms stick up either side of the cage, and they start to expand. As they expand, the elastic cords connecting the cage to the tops of the arms get tighter and tighter.* Finally, the electromagnet is turned off and the cage goes flying up into the air.

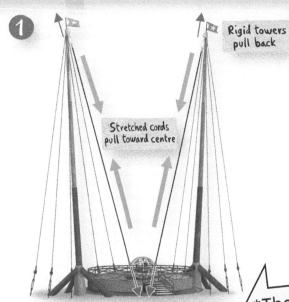

1

Rigid towers pull back

Stretched cords pull toward centre

Cage pulls back

The key forces at the start of a reverse bungee ride. The cage is not moving, which means the forces acting on it are equal. The elastic cord is pulling the arms down with exactly the same force as it is pulling the cage up.

*The cage is now full of potential energy, just like the roller coaster on page 5.

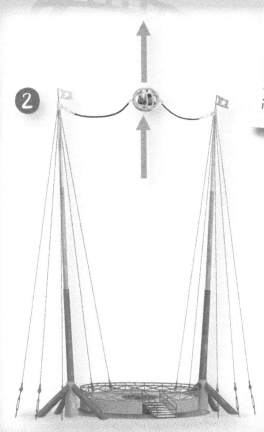

2

The electromagnet is turned off. Suddenly there is no force equal to the pull of the elastic cord, to hold the cage in place. The cage zooms up into the air.

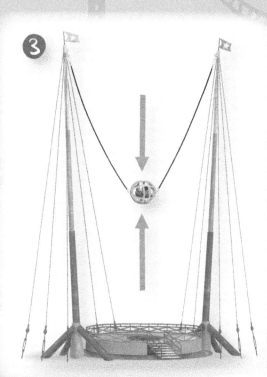

3

The cage bounces down, but not as low as its starting place. There is still no electromagnet pulling it down, and air resistance has slowed it down.

4

Once the cage stops bouncing, the telescopic arm is pulled in, lowering the cage to the ground.

Rotor ride

The giant barrel of fun

When you first walk into the Rotor, it doesn't look very exciting. It's actually a bit like walking into a giant barrel. It's hard to imagine what could be thrilling about this, but once forces get to work, that quickly changes.

What happens inside the Rotor?

You stand with your back against the wall, and the barrel starts to spin. The spinning movement pushes your back against the wall, harder and harder as the barrel spins faster. Then ... *Whoa!* the floor drops away. You're left pinned against the side of the barrel, but instead of being at the bottom, you're halfway up. Only the pressure of your back against the wall keeps you in place.

How do I get down?

At the end of the ride, the Rotor begins to slow down. As it does, the force pushing the riders against the wall becomes less powerful. Instead, gravity becomes the most powerful force affecting the riders, and they slide down the wall. Friction stops them from sliding down too fast and hurting themselves.

The Rotor reaches full speed, and the riders are pushed back against the wall.

1. Electric engine pushes rotor around

2. Engine keeps pushing rotor, so it picks up speed

3. As rotor picks up speed, a force starts to push out from the centre

4. At full speed, riders are pressed against wall so hard that friction holds them in place

The force that pushes people back against the wall of the rotor, is called 'centrifugal force.' When you twirl a ball on a string around your head, you're at the centre and centrifugal force pulls the ball away from you. On the Rotor, though, you are in the position of the ball twirling above your head and not in the centre so you experience centrifugal force as a push.

Wall of Death

Deadly ride

The Rotor (see pages 28–29) *feels* dangerous, but is actually very safe. Another funfair attraction, though, uses similar forces but is *really* dangerous. You could probably work this out for yourself from its name – the Wall of Death.

How does the Wall of Death work?

The Wall of Death is like a giant, straight-sided barrel. It usually measures about 10 metres from side to side. The show goes like this:

1. A motorcyclist rides in circles at the bottom of the barrel.
2. Once the rider has enough speed, he or she rides the bike up on to a ramped section at the bottom of the wall.
3. Picking up yet more speed, the rider goes on to the vertical section of the wall, and rides round and round **horizontal** to the ground.

Sometimes the motorbike carries a passenger. The rider might even invite someone from the crowd to have a go.

Starting a wall of death display, this biker is picking up speed before riding up the wall.

2. As speed increases, centrifugal force gets greater, pushing outward more strongly than gravity pulls downward.

GRAVITY

1. Circular movement, which generates centrifugal force pushing away from the centre of the circle.

Centrifugal force presses tyres hard against wall, increasing friction enough for them to grip.

What makes the Wall of Death so dangerous?

There are two main reasons why it is so dangerous. First, the rider controls the speed of the bike using a twist-grip on the handlebars. Imagine if he let go. The bike would slow down, centrifugal force would become less powerful than gravity, and the rider and bike would plunge to the ground. Second, the tyres are only touching a tiny area of the wall, about the size of the palm of your hand. If they slipped, it would be a disaster.

Glossary

accelerate change the speed at which something is moving. Normally when people talk about accelerating, they mean moving faster

aerodynamic shaped in a way that minimizes the force of air resistance

compressed air air that has been squeezed into a small space so that it pushes outward, for example, air in a bicycle tyre

electromagnet wire coiled around a piece of iron: when electricity is passed through the wire, the iron becomes magnetic (it pulls metal objects toward it)

horizontal level with the horizon (the line between the Earth and the sky)

lift hill first, highest hill on a roller coaster ride

piston one of the moving parts inside an engine, which moves up and down to drive the vehicle along

potential energy object's ability to do work because of its position or shape. For example, a pulled-back catapult has potential energy because its shape is stretched and wants to return to normal size

spherical circular in shape

velocity combination of speed and direction

Index